Gaudí

Text: Enric Balasch

EDICIONES
Aldeasa

Gaudí

◄ Park Güell. Detail of *trencadís.*

An aesthete of architecture

The figure of the distinguished architect Antoni Gaudí and his monumental work has become a referent of any visit to Barcelona. The Barcelona of today, that of the Olympic Games and the Forum of the Cultures, the avant-garde Barcelona that raises buildings such as the Agbar Tower, would not be possible without the legacy of the architects and designers who, at the end of the 19th and beginning of the 20th centuries, broke with the established and highly academic aesthetic rules and argued for what was called Modernism, an artistic movement that was developed jointly in several European countries around 1900, as a reaction to neo-classicism. The experts agree that the movement started in Belgium (where it was called *art nouveau*), but Barcelona is the home of the movement's most international representative, Antoni Gaudí.

A man of Catalan romanticism

Antoni Gaudí i Cornet (Mas de la Calderera, 1852-Barcelona, 1926) had his intellectual training in the atmos-

La Pedrera. ▶

phere of Catalan romanticism, a movement that harked back to the spiritualism of the Middle Ages, following the ideas of John Ruskin (1819-1900), the writer and art critic, and of Viollet-le-Duc (1814-1879), the famous French architect who restored the churches of Vézelay, Saint-Denis, Notre Dame in Paris, Saint-Sernin in Toulouse, and the cathedrals of Chartres, Carcassonne, Amiens and Rheims. Gaudí, unable to imagine in his youth that he would surpass the French maestro, would restore the cathedral of Palma de Mallorca and build the last grand cathedral of the modern era, the Expiatory Temple of the Sagrada Familia.

A student at the Higher School of Architecture in Barcelona, he worked while he studied with the architects Fontseré (gate and waterfall in Ciutadella Park) and Francisco de Paula del Villar (Chapel of the Virgin of Montserrat), from whom he learnt the day-to-day practical work on site. After qualifying as an architect, in 1878 he won a council tender to design lampposts for the street lighting. His earliest works are dated from this period, and the influence of Catalan

Bellesguard. Detail of the ceramic bench. ▲

Lamppost in Plaça Reial in Barcelona. ▶

Ciutadella Park. Waterfall. ▶▶

romanticism is clear: neo-Gothic structures, arabised ele
ments, a particular preference for polychrome ceramic decoration, open brickwork and wrought iron work.

While his first constructions were being built, Gaudí
undertook architectural experiments in order to use parabolic arches, which led him to develop a highly personal style
and new technology in the use of stone. In 1883, at the recommendation of Joan Martorell, an architect and friend of
his, Josep Maria Bocabella, under whose initiative construction of the temple of the Sagrada Familia had begun (the
"poor people's cathedral") according to the plans of the
diocesan architect Francisco de Paula del Villar, handed
over the direction of the works to him, a post he would occupy until the day he died. At the same time, he worked on
other projects and all of them feature his characteristic
hyperbolic paraboloids and his original sense of the art of
sculpting and modelling, which created a new architectural
language. Gaudí's architecture, the rationalism of which
made it a precedent of functional architecture, laid the basis
for the modern organic tendencies. Nevertheless, it was not
all praise in his lifetime. The philosopher Unamuno scorned
his rationalism and thought that his work was wild, more
befitting a madman than a respected architect. In contrast,
Ramiro de Maeztu (1874-1936), a writer who supported
Nietzsche's idea of radical individualism, proclaimed the
Catalan artist's genius and stated that only very rarely did a
genius like Gaudí appear in society.

Towards the end of his life, Gaudí moved to live in the
Temple of the Sagrada Familia. He settled in a kind of studio, a small space without comforts or luxuries that was full
of plans, sketches and models of the project that obsessed
him. Those who knew him saw him as a monk, an aesthete
dedicated to the Work of God. And they were not wrong.
One day in 1926 he left his small studio never to return. He
was killed after being run over by a tram. He dressed so
modestly that nobody recognised the brilliant architect until
many hours later.

The passion for aesthetics

Modernism could be described as a movement that
arose from the passion for aesthetics, when the bourgeoisie

Gate of Casa Güell (above). ▶
Theresan College (below).
Detail of the façade of Casa Vicens. ▶▶

reclaimed the Wagnerian idea of art and almost turned it into a liturgy. The maxim at the end of the 19th and beginning of the 20th century "art for art's sake" marked the totality of daily life, and the tendency was to elaborate on it with great care and affection, recovering the essence of the medieval master builders, who had ensured the survival of their talent and personality through their work, work that due to its long construction process they almost never saw completed.

Modernism was called *Modernisme* in Catalonia, *Jugendstil* in Germany, *modern style* in England, *art nouveau* in France, *Nieuwe Kunst* in Holland, *liberty* in Italy, and *Sezession* in Austria: different names for the same concept whose most active centre was in Catalonia.

In the majority of countries this movement was just a passing fashion that affected only certain specialities, such as jewellery and graphic arts, and only in Belgium and Catalonia did it reach its maximum expression in architecture.

Sagrada Familia.   ▲

Interior of temple.   ▶

Sagrada Familia. Nativity Façade.   ▶▶

Modernist Catalan architecture as inspired by the work of the neo-medievalist Elías Rogent (1821-1897), the architect whose most important projects include the University of Barcelona and the Salamanca district in Madrid, although it did include neo-Gothic elements of oriental aesthetics and the use of wrought ironwork into the concept. The main architects representative of Catalan Modernism were Joan Martorell, Lluís Doménech i Montaner, Antoni Maria Gallissà, Enric Sagnier, Antoni Gaudí and Josep Puig i Cadafalch, the latter thought to be the last Modernist architect.

Interior of Casa Milà. ▲

Casa Milà. Terraced roof. ▶

Sagrada Familia from the terraced roof of Casa Milà. ▶▶

The death of Gaudí

On the 7th of June 1926, a tram knocked down an old man who was absent-mindedly crossing Gran Vía in Barcelona. As he was not carrying any documentation to identify him with and his clothes were very modest, he was taken to the public ward of the Hospital de la Santa Creu, which was for the destitute. Hours later, the deacon and one of the architects of the Sagrada Familia found him there, and they immediately identified the injured man as the maestro Gaudí and urged the hospital to move him to a private room where he died three days later. The whole of Barcelona came out into the street to bid farewell to the supposed destitute old man when his body was driven with full honour to the crypt of his beloved temple of the Sagrada Familia, where he was buried.

Religious architecture

Although Gaudí was a deeply religious man, the fact that architecture is an art that totally depends on commissions strongly limited his production in these types of buildings, though not their importance, since among them features the great work of his life and beyond his own life, the Expiatory Temple of the Sagrada Familia, which has given everlasting fame to its author and to the city that hosted and still plays host to the titanic task if its construction.

Sagrada Familia from Avinguda Gaudí. ▸

Expiatory Temple of the Sagrada Familia

The disagreements between the architect from Murcia, Francisco de Paula del Villar, and the main promoter of the Sagrada Familia, Josep Maria Bocabella, meant that the project came under the direction of Gaudí as early as its first stage. In 1881 Bocabella had bought an entire block of the Eixample district to build a temple that, as can be read from the founding event, would be, "an expiatory church (...) for the honour and glory of the Holy Family. To awaken sleeping hearts from their lack of enthusiasm. To exalt the faith. To give warmth to charity. To help the Lord take pity on the country (...). To calm the anxieties of the Holy See. To lead us free of guilt to the presence of God to implore mercy and attain glory...". Villar's design –a poor temple, with a Romanesque crypt and not very lavish Gothic church, but in line with the aesthetics of medieval archi-tecture– did not come up to Bocabella's expectations, and soon

Sagrada Familia. Two details of the Nativity Façade. ▲
Sagrada Familia. Sculptures on the Passion Façade. ▶
Sagrada Familia. Nativity Façade. ▶▶

accepted the recommendation of his friend Joan Martorell to hand over the direction of the works to Gaudí, who took charge of the Sagrada Familia in 1883, just when the pillars of the crypt had been raised and he had reached thirty-one years of age. The first thing he did was to do away with Villar's Romanesque lines and give the future crypt a historicist Gothic style. After completing the crypt in 1891, he began to design the rest of the temple, finishing the apse in 1893. This was followed by the Nativity Façade (1893-1904), where the Gothic lines were reappraised and he decided to give the work parabolic arches.

Gaudí's Sagrada Familia has a medieval arrangement with a Latin cross ground plan (110 by 60 metres), five naves, three cross-aisles, and a head with ambulatory. Of the three main façades, Nativity, Passion and Glory, only the first was built during the architect's lifetime and the other two have been built from the master's sketches but with statuary by contemporary artists removed from the aesthetics that Gaudí marked on the Nativity Façade.

Sagrada Familia. Detail of the bell towers.　▲

Sagrada Familia. Pinnacles crowning the towers.　▶

Visitors in the Sagrada Familia.　▶▶

Gaudí did not plan his design in advance but created as his imagination dictated to him. This explains why the first sketches bore no technical data. An example of this method of building can be appreciated in the development of the towers, symbols of the church and of Barcelona. The project foresaw eighteen bell towers that would symbolise the twelve apostles, the four evangelists, the Virgin and Christ. At the beginning they were square at the base, but as time went by he decided to give them their current rounded form.

Seen in detail they seem like bishop's croziers because Gaudí wanted to symbolise the apostles, and we should not forget the bishops are their heirs. The Sagrada Familia oozes symbolism on all four sides, like the old Gothic cathedrals. Gaudí, like the medieval master builders, did not only want to build a church, but also wanted to write a catechism on stone, an everlasting text for the memory of the faith and the pride of Christianity.

The Nativity Façade is dominated by the Charity or Christian Love doorway, with the scene of the birth of Jesus and a pelican, the symbol of eternal love. On the left is the Hope doorway, with the saddest events in Jesus' childhood: the slaughter of the innocents and the flight from Egypt.

Finally comes the Faith doorway, with biblical scenes, such as the Annunciation to Mary. This façade is accompanied by four towers dedicated to the apostles Bartholomew (the first to be completed, 1925), Simon, Judas and Matthew, which speak of the importance of the Christian faith. Gaudí wanted to speak of this faith in each and every stone, in the symbols mentioned that refers to both the exoteric and esoteric knowledge of the work. César Martinell, on referring to Gaudí's architecture, writes: "Within these norms –those of Modernism– there is an architectural style in Catalonia that did not eventually have an ethnic personality and which should really be studied due to the particular way that each architect has developed it, which ranges from the total freedom of forms to a deliberate containment and respect for a previously chosen specific style. For Gaudí Modernism was (…) the open (…) door through which he expanded his powerful personality and creative strength…".

Gaudí did not see his *opus magnum* completed. For a long time he thought he could finish the temple in ten years

Pinnacles of the towers (above). ▶

Agbar Tower from the Sagrada Familia (below).

Sagrada Familia. Nativity Façade. ▶▶

on the condition that he could have the 360,000 pesetas promised annually. The financing, however, was not subject to a budget, but because it was an expiatory temple it was built with the donations of the faithful. As a result, the works were interrupted during the First World War. In 1925, as mentioned above, the tower devoted to the apostle Bartholomew was finished, but after the death of the architect the works came to a standstill, with the difficulties in interpreting the plans and the extremely high construction costs contributing to this. However, perhaps as a posthumous homage to the brilliant architect, the three remaining towers were finished by his collaborators.

In 1936, during the Civil War, some plans were lost and a plaster model was seriously damaged by a fire. The works came to a standstill again, but started up again from 1952 by interpreting the surviving plans, although in a very free way. Today the east façade has been finished, but there is still a lot of work to be done. The west façade has

Detail of the vault openings. ▲
Interior naves of the Sagrada Familia. ▶
Agbar Tower from the inside of the temple (above). ▶▶
View from the central nave (below).

also been continued in line with Gaudí's plans, but the complicated nature of the structure, the occasional lack of funds and diverse technical and bureaucratic problems have extended the work for over thirty years.

The critical voices have intensified. Some argue that it should remain unfinished while others want it completed, and meanwhile the oldest sections have already had to be cleaned and restored. But it is a church par excellence of the people of Barcelona, a universal symbol of Barcelona, and while the towers take shape and height the enthusiasm grows and all expectations are that, not counting unexpected setbacks, the Sagrada Familia will some day be completed. Then, whoever has the luck to visit it will see it without scaffolding, cranes, gangways or building material and will be able to appreciate the latest European cathedral in all its splendour. If the architect's desire is satisfied, the opening mass will be heralded in by the voices of 1,500 singers in the choir stalls, 700 children and five organs.

La Sagrada Familia always amazes people. ▲

The towers of the Sagrada Familia form part of Barcelona's landscape. ▶

Many people visit the unfinished temple every day. ▶▶

The Theresan College

This college, built between 1888 and 1889, has few decorative elements in line with the austere spirit of the Order of Saint Theresa that had its main centre here. When Gaudí was entrusted with the construction he was not yet as religiously fervent as he would be years later. He was not sure whether to accept the job or not, because he was used to working without the restriction of money. He had already built Casa Vicens and the Palau Güell, and the wealth of their owners enabled him to work without the need to keep to a strict budget. In this work, however, money counted and counted for a great deal. The Theresan nuns did not have a lot of money and neither did they want a lavish building that would put into question the austerity of the Order. Gaudí tried to stick to his budget but overspent and had to suffer the anger of the priest in charge of the order. Without batting an eyelid, Gaudí stood staring at him and replied, "Each to their own, father. I build houses and you give Mass and pray". The cleric's protestations were based on the bills for the bricks and for the extravagance that he thought it was to decorate the top of the façade with the crenellated brick crest, recalling Gothic style that had no other use than aesthetic. But he was mistaken: Gaudí left nothing to chance and the battlements on the roof had to be for placing symbolic elements such as the doctoral mortarboards that refer to Saint Theresa as the first Doctor of the Church. The centre of the gallery houses the order's heraldic signs, the initials of Saint Theresa are reproduced six times on the wrought iron grilles, and the stone wall that separates the upper floors has a strip decorated with ceramic plaques bearing the name of Jesus.

When Gaudí accepted the job to build the college, the main centre of the order was already standing but, as occurred in Casa Batlló, it did not seem to bother him and once again he stamped his own personal mark on the building. To underline the architect's genius we should mention the fact that the ground plan was divided into three narrow parallel strips, the basement, a long corridor, extended along the central axis of the building, and the ground floor had small courtyards to allow light into the rooms. In normal conditions a similar structure would have needed two transversal support walls, as can be seen in the ground floor, built before Gaudí took over the work. The architect transformed the layout of the upper floors in an extraordin-

Theresan College.   ▶

ary way, however, and in their place built long symmetrical corridors with parabolic arches that enabled him to hold the rest of the building. Through these arches he was able to eliminate the interminable support walls. The white-painted arches that make up these corridors give the collage great distinction, and give off the sensation of penetrating a narrow vault of Gothic ascendancy. The arches are also separated by large windows open towards the inner courtyard so that the corridors receive natural light. Now on the outside, the austerity of the lines are emphasised by a large façade in brick and narrow windows. Nevertheless, a series of pointed arches of diverse sizes remind us that the building is the work of a master architect.

Theresan College. General view. ▲

Entrance gate. ▶

Interior corridor with parabolic arches. ▶▶

Collaborative work with Eusebi Güell

A unique example of the enlightened industrialist, Eusebi Güell was an enterprising man whose industrial initiative and political activities made him one of the most important figures in booming nineteenth-century Barcelona. But he was also a refined sponsor who used his massive fortune to promote all types of art forms, although it was his undying support for Gaudí that gave him most notoriety, since without his generous financing we would not have a large part of Gaudí's work that is still preserved in the city and the surrounding area.

Dragon of Park Güell. ▸

Park Güell

In 1900, Eusebi Güell, Count Güell, commissioned Antoni Gaudí to build a garden city along the lines of the English residential areas. For this project he had the Muntaner de Dalt estate, a piece of land he owned in north-east Barcelona, 150 metres above sea level, to the left of Mount Carmel and to the right of the then village of Vallcarca. The state measures 15 hectares on an irregular surface of gentle slopes that ends in a natural wall. At the top of the hill in the south-west of the property is the area that should have housed the church of this unique garden city, with wide avenues suitable for carriages to pass by, paths shaded by palm trees, benches in the shadiest corners as protection against the sun, viewpoints, Babylonian gardens, grottoes, pathways (3 km cross the park), gentle slopes, bridges made of high arcades, and many more details.

Eusebi Güell, the grand patron

You could say that a large part of Gaudí's work was possible thanks to Eusebi Güell, a man who was committed to art and the artists of his time. As well as Gaudí, Güell gave support to the poet Picó, the writer Pin, the painter Clapés and the musicians García Robles and Rodríguez Alcántara. Eusebi Güell (Barcelona, 15th of December 1847 – 9th of July 1918), the first Count of Güell, studied in England and after graduating took over the factory founded by his father, Joan Güell Ferrer. An untiring traveller, he devoted his time to studying physical and natural laws and was interested in industrial progress. He married Isabel López Bru, daughter of the first Marquis of Comillas, who had eight children by him. Elected district councillor for Barcelona in 1875 and provincial representative in 1878, he also chaired the Centre Català and was a member of the Armed Alert organisation of Catalonia. He belonged to several company boards and founded the Asland cement factory, which still operates today. He developed a large wine-producing centre on his Garraf estate and on his land in the Prades range, where he cultivated vineyards that produced a ferruginous taste that the people of Barcelona liked a lot. A much-loved personality, on his death he was given the honour of mayor, a post he always refused while alive.

Ceramic medallion on the wall of Park Güell. ▲

Stairway at the entrance to the park. ▶

The Fly Agaric

The fly agaric (Amanita muscaria), a poisonous and hallucinogenic mushroom that is common on the peninsula, is represented on the entrance pavilions of Park Güell. For José María Garrut this is not the mushroom in question, and Gaudí was inspired by the sets of the opera Hansel and Gretel, by Engelbert Humperdinck, which was performed in the Gran Teatre del Liceu. However, other writers argue that it is in fact this mushroom, which Gaudí ate to avoid the rheumatic pain that tortured him. Supporters of this theory claim that Gaudí's architecture is the result of the hallucinations caused by the atropine contained in the mushroom. It has never been proven that Gaudí ate this mushroom, but its use by the Catalan peasantry for medicinal purposes is very deep-rooted.

This giant garden was divided into sixty triangular sites on the side of the mountain in such a way as to ensure however many buildings were placed there later, they would never be without the views over the city. The sites measured between 30,000 and 35,000 spans, and the land available for building could not exceed one sixth of the total space, but the plots were expensive since they were in a suburban area of Barcelona that then lacked the essential means for self-sufficiency.

Only the first two houses were built, and the entrance stairway, some pavilions and the wall that closed off the garden city to give a feeling of security to its future dwellers, and the plan failed miserably because only two sites were sold. Nevertheless, Gaudí went to live in Park Güell (written in English as the ceramic medallions on the entrance read) to be able to control the work better and because his ageing father, who was ninety-three years old, was unable to walk up stairs. He lived there until he moved to the Sagrada Familia. After the death of Eusebi Güell, the

Pavilion at the entrance of Park Güell (pages 34 and 35).

Barcelona from Park Güell. ▲

Park Güell. ▶

estate became the property of the city and it was turned into a public park.

In this garden Gaudí showed his sensitivity towards nature in a time when the word ecology was still not recorded in the dictionary. To avoid having to level out the land, he designed pathways, streets and avenues on the edge of the slope using arcades, and the columns were cut with stone from the site so that the harmonious aesthetics of the landscape would not be broken. These artistic and environmental values led UNESCO to declare Park Güell as a World Heritage Site in 1984.

The entrance is watched over by two pavilions that seem to have been plucked from a theatrical set. One can speak here of a delirious architecture, of houses from a fantasy world, of a dream-like rather than real project. The buildings are built of ochre-coloured stone with roofs covered in polychrome glazed tiling. One of the pavilions has a slender

The washerwoman's arcade. ▲
Detail of the washerwoman's arcade. ▶
The park conserves its lush vegetation. ▶▶
View of the park from the central square (page 40).
Undulating bench and washerwoman's arcade (page 41).

Detail of undulating bench (above). ▲
Main square and undulating bench (below).
Trencadís. ▶
Medallion on the stairway. ▶▶

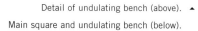

tower (10 m high) covered in blue and white glazed tiles. To make the mosaics Gaudí had the support of Josep Maria Jujol, a well-established master ceramist. After crossing the entrance area a large stairway rises up divided into two sections leading to the higher part of the park. A salamander or dragon with multicoloured scales pours water from its mouth into a small pond. There is a hidden cistern behind this salamander or dragon, with a capacity for twelve thousand litres of water, used for watering the gardens.

Climbing the stairway we come to a portico of columns in Doric style that hold up a roof that is a terrace, the Main Square of the garden city. The railing of this terrace does not only have the function of protecting people from falling but is also a dragon's tail, forming a bench that curves around the square. Both the seat and the back fit the human anatomy to perfection, because Gaudí used a naked man to model on a plaster mould in order to achieve the perfect form that he later passed on to this bench. To decorate it he used fragments of ceramic and glass, a decorative

Washerwoman's arcade (pages 44-45).

Hypostyle Hall. ▲

Musicians in the Hypostyle Hall. ▶

technique that is repeated in many more of his works. The best advice that can be given to a visitor is to lose themselves in the park's rough tracks, and you will almost certainly discover magical spots, full of peace and calm.

Palau Güell

Despite its architectural importance, this building is passed unnoticed by many visitors. Whoever walks along Carrer Nou de la Rambla will confirm that it is practically impossible to see Palau Güell in its totality, and much less get an idea of the richness of its architecture since the façade is generally speaking rather sober in outline.

In 1885 Eusebi Güell commissioned Gaudí to build a palace for him as a residence. The bourgeoisie of the time competed with one another to possess the most luxurious mansions and a man of the standing of Count Güell, whose

Park Güell. Undulating bench (pages 48-49).

Terrace of Palau Güell (above). ▲

Entrance gate (below). ▶

Façade of Palau Güell. ▶▶

fortune had been amassed by his forebears in America, had to be at the head of the pack. Money was no problem to him and he encouraged Gaudí to think more about his architecture that about the costs involved. With this situation, work had hardly begun when the budget was surpassed so much that the count's accountant stated, "While I fill up Don Eusebi's pockets, Gaudí empties them".

The count had a special preference for Gaudí's architectural talent, especially after seeing his projects for the Universal Exhibition of Paris. A man of extraordinary wealth, he wanted a unique palace without worrying about the cost that it would involve. For these purposes he bought some land in Carrer Nou de la Rambla which, due to its relatively small size, needed more than twenty projects to decide on the façade. The main adornment comprises a gallery that projects out from the first floor, diverse sculptural ornamentation, and a column with the Catalan coat of arms between the entrance doors. These doors are closed by two wrought iron gratings inscribed in the interior of the arches they form. Here is an example of the so-called "catenary arches" that he would introduce into many of his later works (the Theresan College, for example). In its time, the "extravagance" of the doors caused a sensation in Barcelona and many people went past the palace to take a look.

The true majesty of the palace, however, is discovered on entering. The play of lights enhance the elements as another crucial aspect of the architecture, and the Modernist pieces are repeated in a decoration full of columns, pillars, marbled coverings, ceramics, noble woods, wrought iron pieces, etc. Gaudí wanted to give the palace a sense of grandeur, despite being built on a small site.

The courtyard of the main floor, perhaps the most stunning and elaborate, has a dome over scallops perforated by circular holes which is erected at almost eighteen metres in height, giving the sensation of a Gothic cathedral more than a palace for civil use: Count Güell held his society parties in this hall, and as a great music lover he commissioned Gaudí to provide it with a unique musical instrument, an organ designed by the architect himself, the pipes of which were on the upper floor, so it seemed as if the music was coming down from heaven: a surprising effect that could only occur to a genius with the talent of Gaudí.

The roof was never a secondary element for Gaudí, as can be seen in many of his interventions. Palau Güell is crowned by a central tower and the chimney and ventilation ducts take in the form of pinnacles, decorated with the typ-

The *trencadís* technique
The delicate ceramic coverings that decorate many of Gaudí's works are given the Catalan name of *trencadís* (brittle). It comprises a mixture of broken pieces of glazed tiling and fragments of glass joined with mortar. With the trencadís technique, never previously used, Gaudí was almost a quarter of a century ahead of the collage technique proposed by the Dadaist movement.

Crowning of a chimney in Palau Güell. ▲

Two of the palace's chimneys. ▶

ical *trencadís,* where one can already get an idea of the towers that he produced later for the Sagrada Familia. He decorated the rooms of the palace with coffered ceilings in eucalyptus and cypress wood completed with trellises that act as supports. The palace was fitted out with furniture of the purest Modernist styles.

Casa Güell or the Güell Estate

Parallel to the building work on the Palau Güell, Count Güell commissioned Gaudí to rebuild and fit out a house on an estate he owned on the outskirts of Barcelona, between Sarrià and Pedralbes. In those days the members of the bourgeoisie competed with each other to show off their personal luxury and external symbols of power were highly valued. With this in mind, one can appreciate why Count Güell gave special consideration to the entrance to the estate and the gate.

Outside of Casa Güell.   ▲
Detail of the ornamentation.   ▶
Entrance to Casa Güell.   ▶▶

For the reconstruction of the pavilions, Gaudí was inspired by the Mudejar style that he had already used on Casa Vicens, his first work. This ornamental unity enabled him to create a homogenous whole in a series of buildings that in principle were very different from each other: the stables, the riding school or porter's lodge.

The porter's lodge, with an octagonal ground plan, is covered by a lowered dome, a technique not used until then by the architect. The outer walls of the stables, an anodyne construction, were covered with ceramics that give the walls a touch of distinction. The riding school, placed alongside the stables, has a graceful dome with an Arab-inspired tower. The riding school and porter's lodge towers act as a transitional element between the two buildings of different styles. The stables show the typical catenary vaults that the architect would use in many more of his constructions.

Nevertheless, the best representation of Gaudian style is in the doorway that separates the lodge from the stables. It is a wrought iron work in the purest Modernist style. The gate

Domes on the pavilions of Casa Güell.   ▲

Medallion with the owner's initials.   ▶

Entrance gate of the estate.   ▶▶

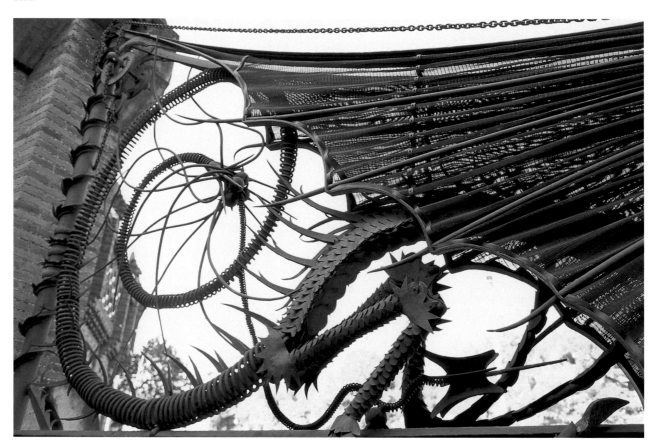

to the doorway, a single piece five metres wide, is attached to a side post more than ten metres high crowned with a floral adornment. The most common thing to have done to avoid such a large load of weight on one side would have been to divide it into two panels, but Gaudí thought that this would make it look like one was entering a prison and rejected this possibility. Standing out on the gate is a dragon that is threateningly opening its mouth. This dragon gives the gate its name and, like other elements, points to the importance of symbols in his later works. The dragon of the Güell Estate speaks in symbolic key of Ladon, the monstrous dragon with one hundred heads that spoke many languages, and watched over the entrance to the garden of the Hesperides where it guarded the golden apples, in line with the typical model of the snake guarding the paradises. This house has become the head offices of the Cátedra Gaudí centre.

Gaudí and alchemy

Some scholars believe that Gaudí embraced the teachings of the Order of the Temple full of alchemic meanings. If we observe the heavy symbolism of his work then this theory has some basis of truth. Gaudí used medieval symbolism in many of his works. For example, the dragon on the gate of Casa Güell refers to Ladon, the monstrous dragon with one hundred heads that guarded the entrance to the garden of the Hesperides, in line with the typical model of the snake guarding the paradises.

Güell Bodegas

On the road between Barcelona and Sitges, crossing over the Garraf massif, today the Garraf Natural Park, a protected area with magnificent scenery and Mediterranean

Entrance gate of Casa Güell (pages 58-59).
The gate is an exquisite piece of wrought ironwork. ▲
Detail of the dragon guarding the gate. ▶

vegetation whose greatest exponent, the *margalló* (palm heart), colonises large areas, are these wine cellars that do not often feature in the Gaudí catalogues because for a long time it was attributed to Francesc Berenguer i Mestres, one of his friends and collaborators.

Eusebi Güell, once again, commissioned his friend and favourite architect Antoni Gaudí to build some wine cellars on an estate he owned in the Garraf region, a work that required six years to complete, between 1895 and 1901. The confusion about which architect was actually responsible for the design is understandable, because its architecture does not fit in with the aesthetic lines that Gaudí stamped on all his works. The combination of rough stone blocks with simple brick pavilions creates a strange mixture of styles that, while breaking the unity, act to create independent spaces and, at the same time, an eclectic decoration in terms of the construction materials.

There are no clear signs that we are before a work by Gaudí. Remember that in his early constructions, such as

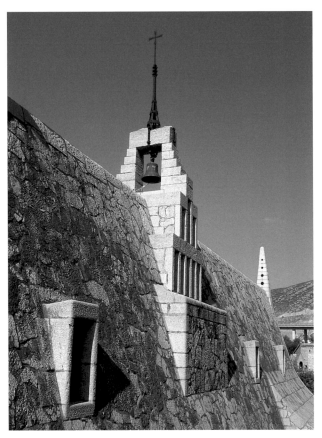

Güell Bodegas. ▲

Crowning of the chapel. ▶

Entrance to the bodegas. ▶

Casa Vicens, although he used Mudejar art, he clearly left signs of the personality of his style. The same does not occur here, there are no Mudejar traits or the typical ceramic decoration that he repeated endlessly in his later works, or even the undulating lines that expressed movement that came out of inertness. There are just two details that enable us to discover the hand of the master Gaudí: the parabolic arches, which rise up to hold vaults, doorjambs of windows, or quite simply, as entrance arches, and the roof, an element that seemed to obsess Gaudí, despite being the least seen part of houses. In the Güell Bodegas the roof is extended until almost reaching the sky, giving the sensation of being in a stone tent. The lodge also has the stamp of the artist: the front door is made up of iron chains. The home, situated above the bodegas, frames the chapel built just above. In the Güell Bodegas it seems that Gaudí had not wanted to be noticed.

Crypt of the Colonia Güell

Just 17 km from Barcelona, in Santa Coloma de Cervelló, a town situated in the Baix Llobregat county, a remarkable

The building is surrounded by Mediterranean vegetation (above). ▲

Medieval-inspired tower (below).

The roof is the most singular part of the Güell Bodegas. ▶

work built between 1808 and 1915 by Gaudí is preserved. Eusebi Güell once again commissioned the distinguished architect to build a church with its corresponding crypt to meet the religious needs of the industrial village of a factory he owned, in Santa Coloma de Cervelló. Count Güell commissioned the design of the houses in the village to two other architects, Francesc Berenguer (who in fact never actually qualified as an architect) and Joan Rubió, but he preferred to entrust the church, a much more delicate project, to Antoni Gaudí.

Gaudí began the works in 1908, just after completing Casa Batlló and having already started on Casa Milà, but due to diverse problems he had to stop working on the project in 1915. Out of the whole church project, only the crypt was built, but the plans and sketches preserved give us an idea of the size of the project, which gives us an inkling of the future forms of the Sagrada Familia and takes elements from previous constructions. The drawings show a church crowned by several towers whose predecessors can be seen in the parabolic arches of the Palau Güell. The lower part

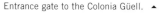

Entrance gate to the Colonia Güell. ▲

Entrance to the industrial village. ▶

has an undulating line that recalls the winding bench of Park Güell, and the columns, leaning in the way of a base, recall those in the Hypostyle Hall of the park.

The works on the crypt lasted almost seven years because Gaudí used this construction as a laboratory of architectural techniques to study the pressures that buildings withstood. To do this he manufactured a scale model made up of small bags of pellets with the proportional weight which, in his opinion, the arches and pillars would have to withstand, and attached them to threads that were the equivalent of the building's structure. In this way he was able to design the leaning columns that are repeated in many of his works.

The crypt is notable for the brick columns, the basalt blocks and stone mixed with lead at the joints. As you walk towards the altar the columns incline in such a way as to give the impression that the whole thing is going to collapse at any moment. It is interesting to see how, in this forest of columns, just like the trees outside, not one of them has the same shape. Gaudí, once again, tries to imitate nature or integrate his work into it as much as possible, since he was always aware that nature was the Creator's crowning work. This respect for nature is patently clear in the stair-

Entrance portico to the crypt of Colonia Güell (pages 68-69).
Detail of the portico vault (above). ▲
Stained glass window of the crypt (below).
Crypt entrance. ▶

way that leads to the crypt. An old pine tree grew there that the architect would not allow to be cut down and changed the structure of the stairway, adapting it to the circumference of the tree: "A stairway can be built immediately," stated Gaudí, "but a tree needs time to grow".

An arched brick vault covers the altar which gives the sensation of entering a grotto, a symbol of the mysteries of Mother Earth, Gaea, which Gaudí admired so much, as the anecdote shows. The crypt cause an emotional unsettling, a feeling of entering into a spiritual world, into the mysteries of Gaea. Puig i Boada, who knew Gaudí personally, describes the crypt in Colonia Güell in this way: "A visitor standing at the foot of the entrance chancery and facing the presbytery can take in the whole interior of the church of Santa Coloma almost in one glance. They will appreciate the view of the apse with the presbytery and altar, and thus be able to carefully follow the divine offices, with their look set on the altar table, thanks to an architectural structure constantly focused on this point, with an interior view that the columns do not interfere with due to their slenderness in both extension and height (…). The observer will see the domes of the central nave, the half-domes of the side naves, the low vaults from which they branch out and the perimeter walls…".

Gaudí never finished this great project which, if it had been, would have been classified as a small Sagrada Familia. After the work was interrupted he devoted himself full-time to the Sagrada Familia until his death.

Interior of the crypt of Colonia Güell. ▶

Spaces for living

As is common for architects, many of the commissions that Gaudí was given throughout his career were for houses for the wealthy and cultured Catalan bourgeoisie of his time, who generally speaking did not obstruct the architect's wild imagination. Today the Gaudian residential buildings in Barcelona form an important series scattered around different districts of the city, particularly in Eixample, where the name of Gaudí is associated with other architects who turned this area into the most unusual laboratory of Modernist style.

Inner courtyard of Casa Milà. ▸

Casa Milà

The last civil work by Gaudí, after which he would devote himself exclusively to the Sagrada Familia, was completed in 1912, and from then to this very day does not cease to amaze whoever looks at it. Located in a central point of Barcelona, on the corner of Carrer Provença and Passeig de Gràcia, hundreds of local people and visitors pass alongside it every day and it is something unavoidable, whoever it is, to stop and look up, if only for a few seconds, to take in the undulating façade of La Pedrera (the quarry), the name that the people of Barcelona of the time gave to Casa Milà because it looked like a sheer wall in their eyes. Restored quite recently, it shows off its beauty and has recovered the grey tone that for years was hidden by a black layer of pollution. The wrought iron work has been painted and rehabilitated, and the broken ceramic pieces have been replaced. The interior, which housed a bingo hall, has been rebuilt in all its splendour. Today the building is the

Front door of Casa Milà. ▲

Detail of the front door. ▶

La Pedrera seen from Carrer Provença. ▶▶

A perfectionist spirit

One could say that Gaudí was a slave to his own creative spirit. A total perfectionist, he never wanted to alter his plans if this meant his work would suffer an unplanned aesthetic change. So when he built Casa Milà, in Passeig de Gràcia, one of the columns of the façade projected one metre into the pavement and passers-by complained about it. The City Council took notice of the complaints and, faced with the impossibility of eliminating the columns (the work was at an advanced state) they allowed it to occupy the pavement on the condition that the upper part was sectioned. Gaudí was not prepared to carry out such an aesthetic mutilation of his work, but neither was he looking for a direct confrontation with the authorities. He accepted the suggestion of the Council experts, but on the condition of placing an explanatory plaque so that people would know the true reason for that imperfection. The City Council did not think it was a good idea to place a plaque (at that time Gaudí was already internationally known) and the column stayed as it was in the original project.

home of the Caixa de Catalunya Foundation, which uses it to hold exhibitions and other cultural events.

Gaudí, as in many of his projects, worked with sketches, models and experimented with scale models that he aimed to transfer into the reality of the work itself. The commission from his friend Pedro Milà Camps (his family lived on the first floor), which gives the house its name, came to him at a time of intellectual and architectural maturity. We should recall that from 1883 Gaudí had been working on the Sagrada Familia and religious feelings imbibed his work. Nevertheless, he wanted to build a naturalist house and he achieved it, because the façade of La Pedrera recalls a sea of rolling waves in which the pieces of ceramic simulate the whitish crests of the foam. In the middle of this wild undulation, never previously seen in a residential building, the spaces of the windows and balconies open up without maintaining the verticality of straight lines that befit buildings of this kind. The ground plan also breaks all the aesthetic rules of residential houses developed around an octagonal plan, typical of Eixample. From a technical point of view, worth mentioning is the multiplication of independent support points, in brick and stone, instead of interior support walls parallel to the façade to organise the corridors.

The vestibule, wide enough for carriages to enter, is full of columns, giving the sensation of entering into the hypostyle nave of a cathedral. The stairway gets natural light as a result of the glazed roof, and is adorned with window boxes that make clear Gaudí's intentions to build a house that was strongly linked to nature.

La Pedrera or Casa Milà. ▸

However, the best decorative elements appear on the roof. Once again Gaudí dedicated a great deal of thought to a part of the house not seen by many people. The chimneys and ventilation ducts are turned into medieval knights covered by their helmets and accompanied by a massive four-armed cross covered in white ceramic.

A setback forced Gaudí to abandon the construction of the house and it was not completed, although in reality only a few details were missing. The distinguished architect had wanted to decorate the façade with several dedications to the Virgin (we have already mentioned that he lived in a deeply religious setting) and even thought about crowning the building with a sculptural group comprising the Virgin, Saint Michael, Saint Raphael and two archangels, turning the house itself into a large pedestal for these images. Finally, however, the sculptures were not placed there because Pedro Milà really did not like the idea. Gaudí became angry, abandoned the construction and ended his friendship with Milà. The results of this break can be seen in detail such as the lack of white ceramic

Balconies of La Pedrera (pages 80-81).

Inner stairway. ▲

Vestibule of Casa Milà. ▶

covering on several chimneys, left to a warm golden bareness that provides unexpected chromatic effects.

Despite this incident, a model of Casa Milà was exhibited at the exhibition held in Paris about Gaudí's work in the same year that he left the work unfinished. The following year a special room was given over to Gaudí in the Architecture Exhibition organised in Madrid by the Central Association of Architects, and La Pedrera featured in a place of honour. Paradoxically, this international recognition did not receive the same popular eulogies. Many sectors of society did not like the house and the newspapers of the time include cartoon strips and caricatures about it.

Casa Batlló

The sobriety of Casa Milà is not repeated in this work, which is remarkable for its polychromy and fanciful forms

Casa Milà. Two details of the inner stairway (pages 84-85).

Four-armed cross on the crowning of a chimney. ▲

Chimneys of Casa Milà. ▶

Crowning of chimneys in the form of helmets. ▶▶

of its large windows, balconies and roof. Although the project did not begin from an empty site, with Gaudí having to transform an already standing house, the reform was so total that one can easily speak of a new construction. Josep Batlló Casanovas, a wealthy textile industrialist, wanted to remodel his house in order to bring it in line with the elegance of Passeig de Gràcia, the street it was built in. This decision was almost certainly influenced by the fact that in 1900 Puig i Cadafalch had built Casa Amatller right next door to Mr. Batlló's home. Both houses, wall to wall today form part of one of the most interesting series of Catalan Modernism applied to architecture.

The original Casa Batlló, built in 1877, must have been a conventional building lacking in style which went completely unnoticed in a particularly elegant area that saw luxurious stately mansions being erected day by day. Having decided to change the appearance of his house, in 1901 Mr. Batlló applied for permission from the City Council to demolish it, but after hiring Gaudí to take charge of the project, he was convinced by the architect to change his mind. Gaudí set to work and let his imagination run free, something that Mr. Batlló did not dislike in the least.

To undertake the project he had the cooperation of Jujol, Rubió and Canaletas, among others, who alongside Sugrañes and Bayó would form part of the team that would help him build Casa Milà shortly after. To start with, Gaudí decided to change the façade completely and replace the load wall of the ground and first floors with bone-shaped columns that would enable the light to enter, especially on the first floor, from whose large windows there is a magnificent view of Passeig de Gràcia. These columns extend into others that attach the whole façade over the pavement giving the sensation, due to their large base perimeter, that they are elephant's feet. The large windows remind one of the oval shapes of the cosmic egg, and the bones, calcium in other words, speak of the beginning of life. Once again symbolism is ever-present in Gaudí's work, symbolism that speaks of the artist's deep knowledge of classical esotericism, of the cryptic message that his forebears, the master builders of Gothic and Romanesque cathedrals, left on the stone as imperishable teachings. Gaudí bore witness to that tradition.

He gave the balconies wrought iron railings that simulate masks or helmets, and the roof is made up of a tower

Casa Batlló. ▶

covered in the typical *trencadís* ceramic, crowned by a four-armed cross also in ceramic. The roof, in the form of a crest or backbone of an imaginary dragon, is covered with multi-coloured ceramic tiles or plaques. He covered the façade with polished stone from Montjuïc, whose sandy tone gave it the appearance of being moulded in clay, as if he wanted to show the beginning of creation according to the bible. It could be said that the building resembles a house from a stage set of a children's tale where, due to the script, knights and dragons are required on the scene.

The undulating lines of balconies, large windows and the façade in general continue inside the building, mainly on the first floor, where the Batlló family lived. The entrance stairway is like the backbone of a gigantic dragon or dinosaur, and the ceilings the spiral of a far-off galaxy. The rooms break all the rules of traditional architecture. The first floor plan preserves a magnificent Modernist chimney, covered with refractory ceramic plaques, with benches built into a hearth providing a cosy warm

One of the large windows of Casa Batlló. ▲

Vestibule of the building. ▶

The roof is like the back of a dragon. ▶▶

place to sit and chat, in line with the Catalan country houses, but with an architectural reinterpretation. Gaudí wrote of this house: "Corners will disappear and matter will be revealed with the richness of its astral curves; the sun will shine through its four sides and it will be like a vision of paradise…".

Casa Vicens

In 1878 a brick and ceramic tile manufacturer, Manuel Vicens, commissioned Gaudí to build a summer house on the outskirts of the city, in what is today the district of Gràcia, at that time an independent town. The young Gaudí, who had qualified as an architect in March of that same year, was given his first project. Nevertheless, between being given the task and its conclusion ten long years passed by due to bureaucratic problems, although Gaudí only worked for five years on the house.

Casa Amatller and Casa Batlló (pages 92-93).

Two details of the balconies of Casa Batlló. ▲

Night view of Casa Batlló. ▸▸

The Apple of Discord
This is the name given to the section of Passeig de Gràcia that forms part of the block (*manzana* in Spanish means both apple and block) bordered by Carrer Aragó and Carrer Consell de Cent. Here stand three buildings designed by the best architects of Catalan Modernism that show the diversity of languages that defined the style. On the corner of Consell de Cent is the Casa Lleó Morera, by Lluís Domènech i Montaner, in which the plant motif decoration predominates. Two doors away, Casa Amatller is the work of Josep Puig i Cadafalch (1867-1956), considered to be the first Modernist architect. Of an emphatically historicist style, it takes aspects of different periods, with medieval style in the forefront. Alongside it is Casa Batlló (1907), one of the best examples of the brilliant Antoni Gaudí's highly personal reading of Modernism which, far from clashing with its neighbour, is in fact in perfect harmony with it in volumes and lines.

In his first project Gaudí shows a rather conventional side, although this should be stated with reservations when applied to the distinguished architect. Despite this, his genius can already be seen in all the corners of the construction, and foresees the paths that his great works would follow. Even today Casa Vicens stands out astonishingly amongst conventional buildings and amid a run-down urbanisation with a flash of colour and fantasy.

The house, with abundant glazed tile decoration, has a square ground plan fitted into a site squeezed between buildings in today's Carrer de les Carolines. The respect that Gaudí had for nature led him to give the house a small garden (no longer in existence) protected from the outside by a wrought iron railing. The Santa Rita spring flowed from this site and its mineral-carbonic water was sold using a glass as the measure.

The walls, of natural stone, give the sensation of enclosing something magical, and the bricks, perfectly combined and integrated into the symmetry of the lines, stand out like decorative elements. What really attracts one's attention, however, is the multicoloured façade, created from square glazed tiles that form vertical draught-boards in many parts, in particular the columns and projections. This geometry recalls the typical Arab constructions of the Maghreb. The towers can easily be seen as the minarets of mosques, and the wrought iron railing of the garden illustrates palm tree leaves, giving the sensation of enclosing an oasis. This basic type of palm leaf features among the first manifestations of Modernism. However, the house cannot be described as Islamic in design, as the cherubim of Christian tradition decorating the balcony railing show.

The inside features a sumptuous decoration of glazed tiles, mural paintings and wooden ceilings, in a mixture of styles or artistic forms that, being disparate, at the same time form part of a unity. The smokers' room, a typical room in bourgeois homes where the men would meet and discuss business, is decorated with mocarabes that hang from the ceiling like stalactites. The upper part of the wall is adorned with papier-mâché plaques and the lower half with gold and blue glazed tiles. The dining room, the most luxurious part, can be considered as fully Modernist. Between the beams of the ceiling there are delicate cherry tree branches, and the walls and doors are painted with diverse motifs. Finally, we should mention the false dome in one bedroom that, despite being painted, has the effect of being a sleight of hand to the point of seeming real.

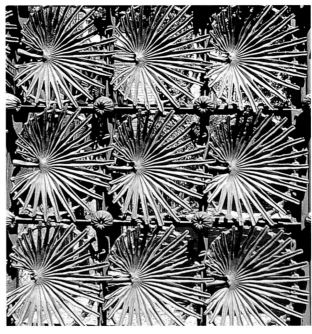

Casa Vicens (above). ▲
Casa Vicens. Detail of the entrance gate (below).
Casa Vicens. General view. ▶

Casa Calvet

Casa Calvet, located in Carrer Casp, in the lower part of Eixample, was built in 1898 as a shop (ground floor) and residence (the high part). These functions restricted Gaudí's artistic freedom and he had to accommodate his architecture to the needs of the construction. He was also forced to create a line of continuity with the already standing buildings, without the possibility of leaving any space open that would allow him to enhance his work. This is why the house seems to be compressed between two blocks and this fact resulted in some complaints from the neighbours, in particular the nuns from an adjoining convent, who lodged a complaint because they considered their privacy was being violated. To avoid problems Gaudí built a trellis in the courtyard that blocked off the view of the convent.

Due to the abovementioned limitations, Casa Calvet is considered the artist's most conventional work, but paradoxically Gaudí received a special mention from the City Council for this project, the only official recognition for his work in his entire life. The experts thought it was rather monotonous. The façade, which in other works of his were heavily decorated and full of fantasy, is sober, even academic here, and only the crowning, made up of two curved pediments, can be called decoration. The roofs, beautifully decorated as we have seen in other examples, are turned into functional elements in Casa Calvet. Only the balconies, with concave iron railings, give the impression of volume and break with the flat symmetry. Over the front door is a baroque-style gallery, and on the entrance are the initials of the family name of the owners of the house, the Calvet family, and a cypress tree as a symbol of hospitality, but also, in the cryptic language that Gaudí dominated to perfection, a symbol of immortality, just like all evergreen conifers.

Even though the lines were subjected to the established rules, the symbols he arranged freely, and through their use we can see how Gaudí left his mark, as occurs with the mushrooms that appear on the first floor, symbolising the interest that Mr. Calvet had in mycology; or the curious doorknocker whose handle hit an insect, representing sin. So when a visitor knocked at the door with the doorknocker, in some way they were self-purifying by punishing and hitting the insect that represented evil.

Casa Calvet. Two genuinely Modernist details. ▸

Casa Calvet. General view of the façade. ▸▸

The inside has twisted columns on the stairway and indigo-blue glazed tiles on the walls, with spiralling motifs that remind one of the creations of William Blake, the British poet, painter and engraver who was a precursor of Modernist ornamentation. Special mention should be made of the furnishing in the house that has been preserved, particularly the doors and metal peepholes, and the furniture designed by Gaudí himself, with curved backs, inclined legs and this undulating symmetry so common in his work clearly here in the backs of the benches and chairs.

Bellesguard or Figueras Tower

Gaudí's Catalan nationalism is quite clear in some of his works, such as the Catalan coat of arms that adorns the entrance to Palau Güell and, particularly, at Bellesguard, a country mansion built for Mrs. María Sagués on the land where Martin I the Humane, the last king of Aragon, had his

Balconies of Casa Calvet. ▲

Cast iron doorknocker. ▶

Inside the hallway of Casa Calvet. ▶▶

castle in the early 15th century. Even before that there had
been a summer residence on the site, built by the king's
widow, Margarita de Prades.

When Gaudí took over the construction of Bellesguard
(beautiful view), between 1900 and 1909, he respected
the very few remains preserved of the old stately home as a
demonstration of his Catalan nationalism and respect for
Martin the Humane. At that time the young architect had
still not defined his style and he built Bellesguard along
Gothic lines, without any artistic concession to Mudejar,
without signs of the Modernism that would have enhanced
it and with a total lack of colour on the outside walls and
façades.

Only the tower, crowned by a four-armed cross, which
can be taken as the author's signature because it features
in nearly all his works, can the touch of the brilliant architect be seen. The rest of Bellesguard, seen from a distance,
seems like a medieval church or perhaps a small fortress in
decline that has seen better days.

Bellesguard. Ceramic bench. ▲

Entrance to the building. ▶

General view of the house and garden. ▶▶

The experts think that Bellesguard does not feature among the best examples of his avant-garde architecture, because it is conventional, predictable and because it follows the model of the Middle Ages; neo-Gothic, however, becomes here a symbol of Catalonia, and we should ask ourselves whether that was exactly what the artist intended or not. María Sagués, the widow of Figueras, a personal friend of the architect, gave him the task of a building that would revive, forgotten by many, the historic value of Martin I the Humane (1356-1410), King of Aragón (1396-1410), son of Pedro the Ceremonious and successor to his brother Juan I, after whose death Castile marked the politics and history of Spain, and Catalonia entered into a period of decline.

In Bellesguard, Gaudí focuses on medieval architecture, builds pointed arches, raises a tower in the style of the old fortresses, the façade has a solid, impenetrable look about it. Only the ceramics decorating the door are a concession to the aesthetic taste of Modernism, but even they have a symbolic value, because they show two blue fish topped by a yellow crown, symbol of Catalonia's maritime power and its Sea Consulate.

The inside, in contrast to the sober, sad outside, has a luminosity that does in fact form part of its aesthetic line. Gaudí built large windows for it and plastered the walls in order to reflect the light better and tone down the forms. The inside contrasts with the outside here perhaps more than in any other of his works. The lines of the sober neo-medieval fortress turn into a Modernist space on the inside with glazed tiling, polychrome glasswork, and smooth and undulating lines. Finally, on the roof there is a pyramidal form that has small arcades. Like many other buildings, however, Gaudí was unable to complete it. This task was undertaken, in 1917, by Domènech Sugrañes.

Miralles Estate

At the beginning of his professional career Gaudí accepted some works of lesser importance to make a living while the world of architecture was opening up to him. One of these works, the only one really worthy of mention, was commissioned to him by his friend Hermenegildo Miralles.

General view of Bellesguard (above). ▶

Medieval-inspired window (below).

Bellesguard. Main entrance. ▶▶

It involved building a doorway for his estate. Gaudí, far from taking the job lightly, designed one of his small master-pieces that are still standing today. We could say that the design of this doorway would be repeated much later, on a bigger scale, in his later constructions such as Casa Batlló or Casa Milà.

Its undulating line extols the architecture of our most internationally acclaimed maestro. In the Miralles estate, Gaudí noted down the first traits of Modernism that would spread in Europe, but also those of surrealism which, after the First World War, had become an ideal aesthetic that extolled everything wonderful, although its most thriving period would be from 1924, two years before Gaudí's death, when André Breton published his *Manifeste surréal-iste*. Gaudí is an architect of Modernism, but in some ways he also wrote the first lines of surrealism applied to archi-tecture.

The door has such curved lines on it that if they became waves then surfing fans would be more than satisfied. The

Mailing that encloses the estate.   ▲

Entrance to the estate.   ▶

Statue of Gaudí facing the entrance.   ▶▶

crowning line curves and practically doubles back, giving a sensation of dynamism, as if the whole piece were really swaying to the rhythm of the waves like a large boat. On one of the sides the arch is extended to become a column that should have housed the Catalan coat of arms. Alongside this column an iron bar railing follows the harmony of the whole, reaching as far as a wall whose undulating top creates an interesting optical effect. A small gable roof crowns the door.

Four-armed cross crowning the door. ▲

Curved crowning of the wall. ▶

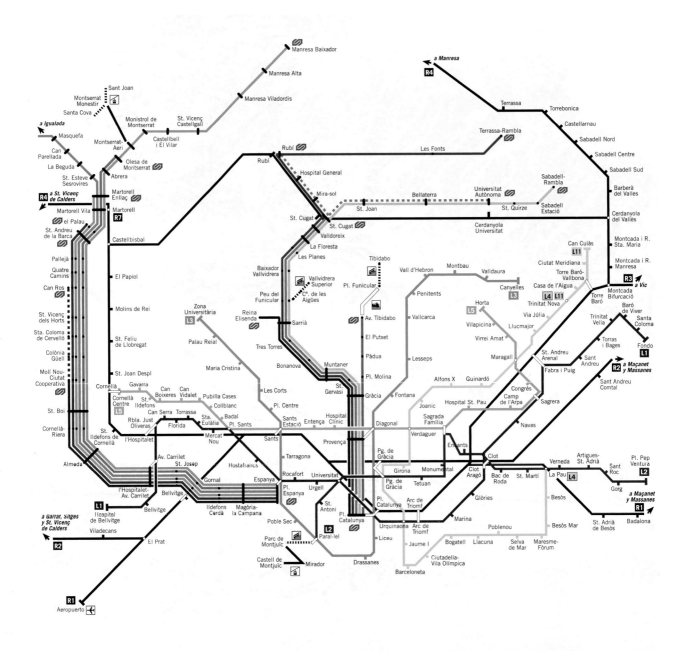

Manresa Baixador
Manresa Alta
a Manresa
R4
Manresa Viladordis
Terrassa
Torrebonica
Montserrat Monestir
Sant Joan
Santa Cova
Monistrol de Montserrat
St. Vicenç Castellgalí
Castellarnau
Terrassa-Rambla
a Igualada
Masquefa
Les Fonts
Sabadell Nord
Castellbell i El Vilar
Sabadell Centre
Can Parellada
Rubí
Montserrat-Aeri
Hospital General
Sabadell Sud
La Beguda
Olesa de Montserrat
Rubí
Barberà del Valles
St. Esteve Sesrovires
Abrera
Mira-sol
Bellaterra
Universitat Autònoma
Sabadell-Rambla
a St. Vicenç de Calders
R4
Martorell Enllaç
St. Joan
St. Quirze
Sabadell Estació
Cerdanyola del Vallès
Martorell Vila
Martorell
St. Cugat
St. Cugat
Cerdanyola Universitat
el Palau
R7
Valldoreix
Montcada i R. Sta. Maria
St. Andreu de la Barca
Castellbisbal
La Floresta
Can Cuiàs
L11
Ciutat Meridiana
Montcada i R. Manresa
Pallejà
Les Planes
Torre Baró-Vallbona
R3
a Vic
Quatre Camins
El Papiol
Baixador Vallvidrera
Vall d'Hebron
Montbau
Valldaura
Casa de l'Aigua
Montcada Bifurcació
Can Ros
Vallvidrera Superior
Tibidabo
Pl. Funicular
Canyelles
L4 L11
Baró de Viver
St. Vicenç dels Horts
Molins de Rei
Peu del Funicular
Cª. de les Aigües
Penitents
Horta
Trinitat Nova
Torre Baró
Santa Coloma
Sta. Coloma de Cervelló
Zona Universitària
L3
Reina Elisenda
Sarrià
Av. Tibidabo
Vallcarca
L3
Via Júlia
Trinitat Vella
Torras i Bages
Fondo
Colònia Güell
L3
El Putxet
L5
Vilapicina
Llucmajor
L1
Molí Nou-Ciutat Cooperativa
St. Feliu de Llobregat
Tres Torres
Pàdua
Virrei Amat
St. Andreu Arenal
Sant Andreu
Palau Reial
Lesseps
Maragall
R2
a Maçanet y Massanes
St. Boi
St. Joan Despí
Maria Cristina
Bonanova
St. Gervasi
Alfons X
Guinardó
Fabra i Puig
Cornellà-Riera
Cornellà
Gavarra
Can Boixeres
Can Vidalet
Pubilla Cases
Muntaner
Pl. Molina
Congrés
Sant Andreu Comtal
Cornellà Centre
St. Ildefons
Can Serra
Torrassa
Collblanc
Gràcia
Fontana
Hospital St. Pau
Camp de l'Arpa
Sagrera
L5
Les Corts
Pl. Centre
Joanic
Navas
St. Boi
Rbla. Just Oliveras
Badal
Sta. Eulàlia
Pl. Sants
Sants Estació
Entença
Hospital Clínic
Diagonal
Sagrada Família
Verdaguer
Florida
Encants
Clot
Almeda
l'Hospitalet
Mercat Nou
Sants
Provença
Clot
Aragó
Bac de Roda
St. Martí
Verneda
Artigues-St. Adrià
Sant Roc
Pl. Pep Ventura
L2
Av. Carrilet
St. Josep
Hostafrancs
Tarragona
Pg. de Gràcia
Monumental
La Pau
L4
l'Hospitalet-Av. Carrilet
Gornal
Rocafort
Universitat
Pg. de Gràcia
Tetuan
Clot
Aragó
Gorg
a Maçanet y Massanes
R1
Bellvitge
Espanya
Girona
Arc de Triomf
Glòries
Besòs
St. Adrià de Besòs
Badalona
L1
Hospital de Bellvitge
Bellvitge
Ildefons Cerdà
Magòria-la Campana
Pl. Espanya
Urgell
St. Antoni
Pl. Catalunya
Urquinaona
Arc de Triomf
Marina
Poblenou
Besòs Mar
a Garraf, Sitges y St. Vicenç de Calders
Viladecans
Poble Sec
Paral·lel
L2
Pl. Catalunya
Liceu
Jaume I
Bogatell
Llacuna
Selva de Mar
Maresme-Fòrum
R2
El Prat
Parc de Montjuïc
Drassanes
Barceloneta
Ciutadella-Vila Olímpica
Castell de Montjuïc
Mirador
R1
Aeropuerto

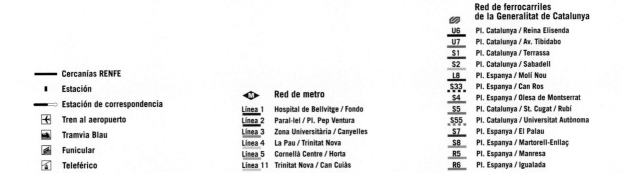

Cercanías RENFE
■ Estación
Estación de correspondencia
✈ Tren al aeropuerto
Tramvia Blau
Funicular
Teleférico

(M) Red de metro

Línea 1 Hospital de Bellvitge / Fondo
Línea 2 Paral·lel / Pl. Pep Ventura
Línea 3 Zona Universitària / Canyelles
Línea 4 La Pau / Trinitat Nova
Línea 5 Cornellà Centre / Horta
Línea 11 Trinitat Nova / Can Cuiàs

Red de ferrocarriles de la Generalitat de Catalunya

U6   Pl. Catalunya / Reina Elisenda
U7   Pl. Catalunya / Av. Tibidabo
S1   Pl. Catalunya / Terrassa
S2   Pl. Catalunya / Sabadell
L8   Pl. Espanya / Molí Nou
S33 Pl. Espanya / Can Ros
S4   Pl. Catalunya / Olesa de Montserrat
S5   Pl. Catalunya / St. Cugat / Rubí
S55 Pl. Catalunya / Universitat Autònoma
S7   Pl. Espanya / El Palau
S8   Pl. Espanya / Martorell-Enllaç
R5   Pl. Espanya / Manresa
R6   Pl. Espanya / Igualada

We would like to acknowledge the cooperation of all the entities and people who have made this edition possible.

Published by: Ediciones Aldeasa
Editorial Coordination: Ana Martín Moreno

Text: Enric Balasch
Translation from Spanish: Steve Cedar
Photography: Ediciones Aldeasa Archives
All of the photographs appearing in this guide were taken by **Mike Merchant,** with the exception of the following: **Ignasi Rovira,** 7, 11, 30-31, 47, 78-79. **Oriol Llauradó,** 12b, 13, 24, 25, 42c, 74-75, 88-89 and cover. **José Barea,** 40, 41, 43. **Miguel Raurich/Iberimage,** 90.

Graphic Design: Estudio OdZ
Layout: Myriam López Consalvi
Cartography: Pedro Monzo
Typeset: Lucam
Printed by: Gráficas Palermo

© of the current edition: Ediciones Aldeasa, 2006
© architectural work p.22-23: Junta Constructora del Temple Expiatori de la Sagrada Familia.
ISBN: 84-8003-821-7
ISBN: 978-84-8003-821-8
Registration number: M-2608-2006
Printed in Spain